Trail Eats

By Sarah Kirkconnell and Matthew "Kirk" Kirkconnell
www.trailcooking.com

A Division of Bay Street Communications, LLC

Trail Eats

Published by Bay Street Publishing, a part of Bay Street Communications, LLC.

Copyright © 2009 – 2014 By Sarah Kirkconnell and Matthew Kirkconnell

All rights reserved. No part of this publication may be reproduced in any form, or by any electronic, mechanical, including photocopying, recording or any information storage and retrieval system, without express written permission from the publisher, except for use in reviews.

Trademarks:

All terms mentioned in this book that are known to be trademarks or service marks have been appropriately capitalized. Bay Street Publishing cannot attest to the accuracy of this information. Use of a term in the book should not be regarded as affecting the validity of any trademark or service mark.

Warranty and Disclaimer:

The information in this book is distributed on an "as is" basis, without warranty. Although every precaution has been taken in the preparation of this work, neither the author(s) nor the publisher shall have any liability or responsibility to any person or entity with respect to any loss or damage caused or alleged to be caused directly or indirectly by the information contained in this work. The publisher and author take no responsibility for the use of any materials or methods described in this book, nor any products thereof. Neither the author(s) nor the publisher is offering medical advice.

Other Information:

Cover Design by Sarah Kirkconnell
Cover and interior photography by Matthew Kirkconnell
First Edition: January 2014

Dedication:

To Kirk, thank you for every single time you have dropped off, and picked me up at remote trailheads.
To Dani, for encouraging me often, and helping me out.
To my kids, for being my trail buddies.
To my readers, thank you for reading, sharing and trying my recipes. And for your feedback and comments. The community we hikers and bloggers have built is amazing. I wouldn't have had this amazing part of my life without all of you!

Intro:

Between 2009 and 2013, Kirk and I developed these 50 recipes that really stood out to us, for our outdoor food column, Trail Eats, which ran from 2009 to 2013.
From raw energy bars, to luxury desserts, hearty carb fests and even pizza, we hope you enjoy some of our favorites, while you are out on your adventures!

BREAKFAST

Trail Mochas

Ingredients:

½ cup dry milk

½ cup powdered sugar

¼ cup unsweetened cocoa powder

2 Tbsp instant espresso powder

½ tsp cornstarch or potato starch

Pinch salt

At home:
In a large bowl whisk the ingredients together, for a smooth powder sift it as well. Pack into three snack size bags in ½ cup portions.

To prepare:
Add 1 cup boiling water slowly to the mix, stirring well. Sip away and wake up!

Notes:
Medaglia D'oro instant espresso can be found in the coffee aisle in most grocery stores, look for a green-capped glass bottle.

Carrot Cake In A Bowl

Ingredients:

½ cup old fashioned oats

2 Tbsp diced dried carrots

3 Tbsp brown sugar

2 Tbsp raisins

2 Tbsp dry milk

¼ tsp ground cinnamon

Pinch salt

2 Tbsp shredded coconut

At home:
Whirl the oats in a blender until about 1/3 of the original size. Put them in a quart freezer bag. Process the carrots in the same manner, adding them to the bag along with the other dry ingredients.

In camp:
Bring 1 ¼ cups water to a boil in your pot. Add in the dry ingredients; stirring well and let come back to a boil. Take off the stove, cover tightly and let sit for 5 minutes. Stir well and top with coconut.

Serves 1

Notes:

For a less strong carrot taste only use 1 Tablespoon. For a vegan version, use rice or soy milk powder.

Peanut Butter Granola Cups

Ingredients:

1 large egg

½ cup chunky style natural peanut butter

1/3 cup brown sugar, packed

¼ cup honey or agave nectar

5 Tbsp vegetable oil

2 ¼ cups old fashioned oats

½ tsp ground cinnamon

¼ cup sliced toasted almonds

½ cup mini chocolate chips

Directions:

Preheat the oven to 350°F. Spray a 12-cup muffin tin with cooking spray.

In a large mixing bowl beat the egg with a hand mixer until combined, add in the peanut butter, brown sugar, honey and oil, beat until smooth.

Add in the oats, cinnamon and almonds, stir in by hand, then gently fold in the chocolate chips.

Divide equally between the muffin cups, then press down firmly with your fingers.

Bake for 15 to 20 minutes or until golden brown.

Let cool for an hour, then work a butter knife around each one and gently pop out (taken out while warm increases the chance of crumbling).

Store tightly wrapped.

Notes:

To make vegan substitute:
1 Tbsp flaxseed meal + 3 Tbsp water = 1 egg. Replace the honey with agave nectar (or preferred sweetener of choice) and use organic brown sugar. And use a vegan friendly chocolate chip.

We used Adam's natural peanut butter; any natural style nut butter may be used. Same with the almonds, it is interchangeable.

Brown Sugar & PB Oats

Pack in a quart freezer bag or sandwich bag:

1 cup 1-minute Quick oats

¼ cup dry milk

2 Tbsp raisins or diced dried fruit/berries

2 Tbsp brown sugar

1 tsp ground cinnamon

Also take:

1 packet peanut butter or nut/seed butter (2 Tbsp)

Freezer Bag Method:

Bring 2 cups water to a near boil; add water to dry ingredients, stirring in slowly. Seal bag and let sit for a minute, open and stir well, add in nut butter.

Insulated Mug Method:

Bring 2 cups water to boil, add dry ingredients to a large insulated mug, stirring well. Cover and let sit for a minute, stir in nut butter.

One Pot Method:

Bring 2 cups water to boil, add in dry ingredients, stirring well. Take off heat and let rest for a minute. Stir in nut butter.

Serves 2

Notes:

Justin's nut butter packets are the perfect size, and readily available at most grocery stores and REI stores.

To serve two easily, carry an extra quart freezer bag. Cuff down to make a "bowl", divide oatmeal and enjoy.

Cranberry Pear Compote

Ingredients:

¼ cup dried cranberries

¼ cup dried pears, chopped

2 Tbsp brown sugar

¼ tsp dried orange zest (or a True Orange packet)

Pinch fine sea salt

At home:

Pack the ingredients in a snack bag or pint freezer bag, depending on cooking method.

Insulated Mug/Bowl Method:

Add the ingredients to an insulated mug or small bowl, cover with ¼ cup of water. Cover and let hydrate for 20 to 30 minutes. If a bit dry, add in a little more water as needed.

Freezer Bag Method (FBC):

Bring ¼ cup water to a boil, set aside. Place the freezer bag in a cozy; add the water and seal bag. Let hydrate for 20 to 30 minutes. If a bit dry, add in a little more water as needed.

Serves 2

BARS, BALLS & NOSHES

Chocolate Chia Bars

Ingredients:

1/3 cup Chia Seeds

1 cup Raw Almonds

1 ½ cups pitted Medjool Dates(15 to 25, depending on size)

1/3 cup unsweetened cocoa powder

½ tsp pure vanilla extract

¼ tsp pure almond extract

Directions:
In a food processor pulse the almonds a couple of times, transfer to a small bowl. Add the dates and process until a paste forms. Add the nuts and remaining ingredients in, process until mixed.
Line an 8×8" glass baking dish with plastic wrap, knock the mix out and flatten into the dish, until even, press down firmly.
Cover and refrigerate till cold, cut into bars and store tightly wrapped.

Notes:
Chia seeds can be an odd texture if you are not used to them. To make them finer, grind them in a clean coffee mill first, use as directed above.

Pistachio Truffles

Ingredients:

¾ cup Almond Meal/Flour

½ cup D'Noir Prunes, finely chopped

¼ cup natural peanut butter or favorite nut/seed butter

3 Tbsp pure maple syrup

2 Tbsp semi-sweet or dark chocolate chips, chopped

¼ cup unsalted pistachios, chopped

Directions:
Stir all the ingredients but the pistachios together until well mixed in a bowl. Add the pistachios to a shallow bowl. Use a 1 Tablespoon disher (scoop) to make balls, roll gently in your hands to smooth out, then roll in the nuts, gently pressing them in.

Store wrapped in the refrigerator until trip time, use within 3 weeks for best taste.

Makes 15 balls

Chewy Granola Bars

Ingredients:

1 ½ cups Rice Krispies® or similar cereal

1 ½ cups 1-minute quick cooking oats

1/4 cup raisins

1/4 cup shredded coconut

1/3 cup semi-sweet chocolate chips, frozen

1/2 cup brown sugar, packed

1/2 cup pure maple syrup or honey

1/2 cup peanut butter (preferably natural)

1 tsp pure vanilla extract

Directions:

Spray an 8×8″ glass baking dish with cooking spray.

Mix the cereal through chocolate chips in a large heat safe mixing bowl.

In a medium saucepan bring the sugar and syrup to a boil, take off the heat and add in the peanut butter and vanilla, stir till smooth.

Quickly add the hot syrup to the dry, mixing while pouring in, with a silicone spatula. Stir quickly till the cereal is coated and immediately dump into the prepared pan, pack down firmly with the spatula.

Let sit till cool and then slice into bars with a thin knife, wrap tightly for carrying. How many? Depends on your size of bar!

Note:
Substitute any favorite nut or seed butter for the peanut butter and any small dried fruit for the raisins.

Blueberry Almond Bars

Ingredients:

1 cup Medjool Dates, pitted (15 to 20)

1 cup Raw Almonds

½ cup Dried Blueberries

2 Tbsp natural Shredded, Unsweetened Coconut

1 ½ tsp ground cinnamon

Directions:
Chop the dates up roughly. Add them and the remaining ingredients into a food processor. Pulse until chopped up, run on high for 3 to 4 minutes until finely diced and starting to stick together.
Line an 8″ x 8″ glass dish with parchment paper on the bottom, knock the mixture into the dish and flatten out, pressing down hard to compact it. Cover and refrigerate. Cut into bars of desired size, wrap each bar tightly.

For long term storage keep in the refrigerator, use up in 3 weeks for best taste. These bars are full of fiber, nut protein and chocolate to crave the sweet monster but with no refined sugar (dates give the sweetness).

Cran-Mac Caramel Bars

Ingredients:

12 oz box cereal of choice

½ cup dried sweetened cranberries

½ cup chopped macadamia nuts

1 cup honey

1 cup white sugar

1 Tbsp molasses

1 tsp pure vanilla extract

1 cup natural peanut butter

Directions:
Spray a 9x13-baking pan with cooking spray or butter it. Set aside.

In a large and tall saucepan heat the honey, sugar and molasses till it comes to a full boil. Take it off the heat and quickly stir in the peanut butter and then the vanilla. Mix in the cereal, cranberries and nuts with a wooden or silicone spoon till fully coated.

Dump into the pan and spread out, then pack in tightly. Let cool for at least an hour to set up. Cut into portions and tightly wrap in plastic wrap.

These bars carry well in a pack and do not fall apart as they are dense and nicely sticky.

Makes one tray (bars depend on your concept of a "serving").

Notes:

For the cereal choose a type with texture, flakes and crunchies work well. It doesn't need to be a sweet cereal as the caramel base is sweet enough on its own. If you have a favorite high protein/fiber cereal, by all means use it. Look for a 12 to 13 ounce box preferably.

And of course you can swap in your favorite nuts and dried fruits!

For the peanut butter, crunchy is the best.

Honey Roasted Almond and Cranberries

Ingredients:

½ cup agave nectar or honey

2 Tbsp butter (or margarine if preferred)

½ tsp ground cinnamon

½ tsp salt

3 cups whole almonds (or nut of choice)

6 ounce bag dried cranberries

3 Tbsp granulated sugar

½ tsp ground cinnamon

¼ tsp salt

Directions:
Preheat the oven to 325°F and line a baking sheet with parchment paper.
In a heavy medium saucepan bring the agave or honey, butter, salt and cinnamon to a boil, let cook for 2 minutes, stirring constantly.
Put the nuts and cranberries in a large heat safe mixing bowl, pour the hot syrup over and stir to cover. Spread out on the baking sheet.
Bake for 15 to 20 minutes, or until the nuts are golden. Take out and allow to cool down.
Knock the nuts into a large mixing bowl and toss with the sugar, cinnamon and salt till coated. Spread out on a new piece of parchment paper to finish hardening up.

P'Nut Butter & Granola Bites

Ingredients:

¼ cup honey or agave nectar

1/4 cup natural peanut butter, creamy or chunky

1 cup puffed rice cereal (Rice Krispies© or similar)

3/4 cup granola of choice

Directions:

Spray a 9×5" loaf pan with cooking spray and set aside.

In a medium saucepan heat the honey over medium heat till it comes to a boil. Pull off the heat and stir in the peanut butter. Quickly work the cereals in till coated.

Using a silicone spatula pack the mixture into the pan and press down gently.

Chill in the refrigerator for a couple of hours, turn out of the pan and cut into pieces. Stash in the refrigerator until trip time. Cary tightly sealed in a plastic bag.

Serves 2

Note:

We used chocolate hazelnut granola, use what you like.

Easy Nut and Chocolate Truffles

Ingredients:

½ cup nut butter of choice

3 Tbsp unsweetened cocoa powder

3 Tbsp granulated sugar

2 Tbsp mini semi sweet chocolate chips

1 tsp pure vanilla extract

You will also need for rolling:
Cocoa powder
Mini chocolate chips
Shredded Coconut

At home:
Mix everything in a medium bowl, using a fork to gently combine. Scoop out balls, about 2-teaspoon size of the mix. Roll gently to cover in your topping of choice. Store tightly covered in the refrigerator till trail time.

To carry:
Pack in a small plastic box to protect. A lightweight 'sandwich box' works well and can do double duty as a dinner bowl afterward!

Notes:
We use a 'disher' to do the scooping, these can be found in any well stocked kitchen department. They keep your hands mess free and make evenly sized truffles!
Use any nut butter (or even sunflower butter!) to your liking. Natural style butters (where the oil separates) will result in a softer truffle, where the mixed kind is firmer.

LUNCH

Pistachio Couscous Salad

Ingredients:

2 cups lower sodium vegetable or chicken broth

1 Tbsp diced dried onion

1 ½ cups couscous

15-ounce can chickpeas (garbanzo beans), rinsed and drained

Dressing:

1/4 cup white balsamic vinegar (or white wine vinegar)

1/4 cup extra virgin olive oil

1 Tbsp honey or agave nectar

1/2 tsp ground black pepper

1/4 tsp dried basil

¼ cup shelled and diced pistachios

Directions:

Bring the broth and onion to a boil, in a medium saucepan, add in the couscous. Take off the heat, cover tightly and let sit for 10 minutes. Fluff up the couscous with a fork into a large bowl, toss with the chickpeas.

Whisk the dressing in a small bowl. Pour the dressing over the salad and toss to coat. Let chill overnight, stir in the nuts and then pack into lightweight sandwich containers (such as Glad or Ziploc brand ones). Serves 2-3 large portions

Pecan Cranberry Ranch Chicken Salad

In a quart freezer bag:

½ cup pecans, finely diced

½ cup dried cranberries

Also take:

7 ounce pouch chicken breast

2 packets or tubs shelf-stable ranch dressing

2 large burrito or 4 taco size flour tortillas

Directions:

Add chicken to the pecan bag, stir to coat. Add in dressing to taste, stirring well.

Spread on tortillas and wrap.

Serves 2

Notes:

For a first day out meal, bring along shredded lettuce (find in produce section in small bags) and cheese slices (deli section).

Find tubs of ranch dressing by Hidden Valley in the salad dressing section in grocery stores. For a convenient grab n' go, pick up a bag of Fresh Gourmet nuts/raisins, found in the produce section, usually with the croutons. The bags are resealable and great to just munch on as well. Or you can buy small bags of diced pecans in the baking section. Sahale Nuts in small bags also work well, look in the produce or candy aisle.

Garden Vegetable Couscous

Pack in a quart freezer or sandwich bag:

1 cup freeze-dried vegetable blend

2/3 cup couscous

¼ cup shelf-stable Parmesan cheese

2 Tbsp dry milk

1 Tbsp lower-sodium bouillon powder

½ tsp granulated garlic

½ tsp dried parsley

½ tsp ground black pepper

½ tsp onion powder (not onion salt)

½ tsp turmeric powder

¼ tsp fine sea salt

Also take:

1 packet or 1 Tbsp olive oil

Freezer Bag method:

Bring 2 ½ cups water to a near boil. Place bag in a cozy, add in water and oil, storing well. Seal tightly and let sit for 10 minutes.

Insulated Mug method:

Bring 2 ½ cups water to boil, add in dry ingredients to a large mug, stir in water and oil. Cover tightly, let suit for 10 minutes.

One Pot method:

Bring 2 ½ cups water and oil to boil, add in dry ingredients, stirring. Take off heat, cover tightly and let sit for 10 minutes.

Serves 2

Notes:

Find Just Veggie blend at grocery & natural food stores and REI or substitute with Mt. House freeze-dried vegetables, found in REI. Oil packets, order online via Minimus. Shelf stable Parmesan cheese? Use the green can type (good ol' Kraft), in the pasta aisle.

Hearty Spinach & Artichoke Wraps

Ingredients:

1 burrito size flour tortilla, per wrap (see notes)

1 Tbsp ranch dressing, per wrap

2 slices cheese, per wrap

3 slices deli meat, per wrap

14 ounce can water packed artichoke hearts, well-drained

1/4 cup baby spinach leaves, per wrap

Directions:

At home -

Lay out a tortilla for each wrap. Brush on the dressing. Lay down the cheese, then the meat on top. Squeeze the artichoke hearts gently to remove all water, chop up two hearts per wrap and sprinkle on top. Lay the spinach on top, roll up each wrap tightly. Wrap in plastic wrap and chill. Carry to the trailhead in a cooler, insulated with ice packs.

Notes:

To carry safely on the trail build "ice packs" by putting ice cubes in quart freezer bags. When you get to lunchtime your wraps will be safely chilled and you will have ice/ice water to add to your water bottle! Look for the gourmet tortillas in fun flavors like Sun-Dried Tomato or as well ones sold as wraps in the bread section of the store. Water packed artichokes can be found inexpensively at Trader Joe's, oil packed can be subbed, drain well.

Savory Tuna Salad

Ingredients:

2 packets 2.6 ounce tuna in oil

½ cup sliced olives

2 Tbsp capers, drained

2 Tbsp lemon juice (fresh or bottled)

¼ tsp red pepper flakes

¼ tsp dried basil

2 string cheese sticks (2 ounces)

2 flour tortillas or pita bread

Directions:

At home:
Pack the olives through basil in a quart freezer bag and seal tightly. Pack with everything else.

Directions:
Open the tuna packets and shake into the freezer bag. Slice or shred the cheese and add in, using a long handled spoon to combine. Divide between the bread of choice or eat out of the bag. If feeling the love, carry a small tub of ripe grape tomatoes to go with your lunch.

Serves 2

Notes:
Substitute regular tuna, be sure to add a Tablespoon or two of olive oil in with your olives. Olives and capers carry well for the day, make this for a dayhike or first day out lunch though. If you are interested in making this meal for long term carrying, please visit the dehydration section on our website for the how-to on drying the olives and capers. For the lemon juice you can substitute True Lemon powder. ½ cup sliced olives is one small can worth.

BBQ Chicken Wraps

Ingredients:

7 ounce pouch chicken

2 flour tortillas (soft taco size)

¼ cup BBQ sauce

2 sticks pepper-jack cheese

¼ cup French fried onions

2 paper towels

Directions:
Open up the chicken pouch and add in the BBQ sauce, stirring well to break up the chicken.
Lay out a clean paper towel for each tortilla, divide the chicken between the two. Dice up a piece of cheese on each tortilla, then sprinkle on the onions. Roll up and enjoy!
Take more of the fried onions as a side treat too!

Notes:

BBQ is shelf stable and can be carried in a leak-proof container or you can use two tubs from a fast food restaurant. Pepper-jack cheese can be found at most grocery stores in sticks like string cheese. If you cannot find, carry 2 ounces of the cheese.

Asian Chicken Slaw Wraps

Ingredients:

7 oz pouch chicken breast

4 soft taco size tortillas

2 cups broccoli slaw

1/3 cup natural chunky peanut butter

¼ cup rice vinegar

2 Tbsp lower sodium soy sauce

2 tsp sesame oil

½ tsp granulated garlic

¼ tsp red pepper flakes

At home:
Pack the tortillas in a gallon size freezer bag (they fit perfectly at the bottom of bear canister). Pack the slaw mix in a quart freezer bag. Mix the dressing up till well blended. Carefully put it into a sandwich bag or a plastic container.

In camp:
Open the chicken pouch up and add it to the peanut sauce, stirring in. Pour the sauce over the slaw in the slaw bag. Seal tightly and shake the bag to distribute the sauce. Let sit for 15 to 30 minutes for the flavors to meld, then stir well.
Divvy up on the tortillas, wrap up and enjoy.

Makes 4 tortillas, serves 2

Notes:

Broccoli slaw can be found in most grocery store produce departments in the bagged section. It is crisp and juicy - and holds up well on the trail for days. It often has broccoli, purple cabbage and carrots in it. You can substitute shredded coleslaw mix in as well.

SOUPS & CHOWDERS

Beef Curry Noodle Bowl

In a sandwich bag:

½ cup chopped jerky (regular or peppered taste great)

½ cup dried vegetable mix

¼ cup raisins

1 Tbsp mild curry powder

4 tsp lower sodium beef bouillon

1 tsp granulated garlic

In a sandwich bag:

6 ounce package chuka soba noodles, crumbled

Directions:
Add 4 cups water to your pot with the first bag and bring to a boil. Add in the noodles, return to a boil and let simmer gently for 3 minutes. Take off the stove, cover tightly and let sit for 5 minutes. Season to taste with salt, if desired.

Serves 2 large bowls

Notes:

Chuka soba noodles (also called chow main noodles) can be found in the Asian section of most grocery stores and look similar to ramen but are not deep-fried, in a pinch angel hair can be used.

Chicken and Apple Soup

In a sandwich bag:

1 cup instant rice

1/3 cup chopped dried apples

1/4 cup chopped sun-dried tomatoes (dry, not oil-packed)

1 Tbsp diced dried onion

4 tsp chicken bouillon (regular or lower sodium)

2 tsp mild curry powder

2 tsp dried parsley

1 tsp granulated garlic or garlic powder

Also take:

7-ounce pouch chicken

Directions:
Add the dry ingredients, chicken (with any broth) and 4 cups water to a large pot (2 Liter works well) and bring to a full boil. Take off the heat, cover tightly and let sit for 10 minutes. In cooler weather or at high altitude wrap your pot in a pot cozy.

Serves 2 large or 3 medium servings

Notes:
This soup is an easy last-minute recipe – everything you need can be found at most grocery stores. Find the tomatoes hidden in the produce department (look up high), apples with the dried fruit and onions in the spice section. It can also be made vegetarian by leaving out the chicken and using vegetable broth, just double the tomatoes and apples.

Blustery Day Double Potato Chowder

Ingredients:

1 cup dried instant hash browns

¼ cup diced dried onions

4 tsp low sodium vegetable or beef bouillon

1 tsp dried parsley

¼ tsp diced dried garlic

¼ tsp dried thyme

¼ tsp ground black pepper

½ cup instant mashed potatoes

¼ cup shelf stable parmesan cheese

½ cup fried onions

1 Tbsp olive oil (1 packet)

4 cups water

At home:
In a sandwich bag pack the hash browns through black pepper. In a second bag pack the mashed potatoes through the fried onions. Tuck in the oil.

In camp:
Add the vegetable/seasoning bag and 4 cups water to your pot. Cover and set aside for 15 minutes for the vegetables to rehydrate. Add the oil, stir well and bring to a boil. Lower the flame to low, cover and simmer on a low boil for five minutes. Turn off the stove and the contents of the cheese/potato bag to the pot. Stir well, taste for seasoning and more pepper and salt as desired.

Serves 2

Slide Mt. Bean Chowder

In a quart freezer bag:

1/2 cup instant rice

1/3 cup instant black refried beans

1/4 cup freeze-dried corn

1 Tbsp shelf stable Parmesan cheese

1 tsp diced dried bell peppers

2 Tbsp dried salsa

Freezer Bag method (FBC):

Add 2 cups near boiling water. Stir well, seal tightly and put in a cozy for 15 minutes. Stir again well.

Mug method:

Add 2 cups boiling water to the dry ingredients in a large mug. Stir well, cover tightly and let sit for 15 minutes.

One pot method:

Bring 2 cups water to a boil in your pot. Add in the dry ingredients; stir well and let sit for 15 minutes tightly covered, in cold weather wrap your pot in a pot cozy to retain heat.

Serves 1 as a meal, 2 as a side cup of soup

Notes:

Instant black refried beans are sold in natural food sections of grocery stores, look for bulk or Fantastic Foods brand or use black bean dry soup mix. Freeze-dried corn is sold at many natural food stores and REI, look for Just Veggies brand. Find dried bell peppers in bulk sections of natural food stores. On cold weather trips carry fresh salsa in a tightly sealed snack bag instead of drying it. Salsa is easily dried at home, see our website for more information. To add more calories in winter add a stick of Pepper-jack cheese diced up (find with the string cheese) at the end.

Clam and Bacon Chowder

In a sandwich bag:

1 cup instant plain mashed potatoes

1/4 cup shelf stable bacon

4 tsp low sodium chicken bouillon

1 tsp dill weed

1/4 tsp granulated garlic

1/4 tsp black pepper

In a second bag:

1/4 cup dry milk

2 Tbsp all-purpose flour

Also take:

1 Tbsp or 1 packet olive oil

6.5 ounce can minced clams

1/4 cup shelf stable Parmesan cheese with 1 tsp dried chives mixed in

Directions:

Add 1 cup cold water to the milk bag, seal tightly and shake up till dissolved.

Add 3 cups water, oil and contents of potato bag to your pot. Bring to a boil and stir the milk mixture into the soup. Bring back to a gentle bubble and let thicken.

Turn to a low flame and add in the clams with broth and cheese, let heat through but don't boil.

Impress your eating partner tips: Sprinkle the top of the soup with additional bacon and dill weed, pick up 2 sourdough "bread bowls" at the bakery on the way out of town. Carve and serve the soup in them.

Serves 2

Notes: Oysters (smoked or not) can be used instead. Find lightweight tins in the canned fish aisle. Find olive oil packets at www.minimus.biz

Chicken Stew & Dumplings

In a sandwich bag:

1 cup biscuit mix

1 Tbsp dry milk

1 tsp dried chives

1 tsp dried parsley

Mark on bag "Add 1/3 cup water".

In a sandwich bag:

3/4 cup freeze-dried vegetable mix

1 Tbsp diced dried onion flakes

1 Tbsp diced instant hash-browns

In a small bag:

4 tsp low sodium chicken bouillon

1/2 tsp dried parsley

1/4 tsp dried thyme

1/4 tsp diced dried garlic

1/4 tsp black pepper

Salt to taste

Also take:

7-ounce pouch of chicken

Cover the vegetables with cold water and let soak for 5 minutes in a 2 Liter pot (or bigger).

Add 4 cups water, both the broth and vegetable bags and the chicken with any broth to your pot. Bring to a boil, taste the broth and salt to taste. Lower the heat a bit on your stove and keep simmering at a low boil. Meanwhile mix up the biscuit mix in its bag. Add the water, push out any air, seal the bag and knead till mixed. Snip a corner on the bag and start squeezing out dumplings. Let them simmer on the soup, with lid on for 5 minutes or till the dumplings are steamed and done (poke a spoon in one to check for being doughy), lowering the flame as needed to prevent boil-overs.

Serves 2 large bowls or 3 small bowls

Notes: Instant hash browns are sold with the instant mashed potatoes and Costco. Look for Just Veggies brand dried veggies at Whole Foods, REI and other stores. Dried onions find in the spice aisle and Costco.

DINNERS

Fish Tacos

Bring:

2 5-ounce pouches Albacore tuna or salmon

1 Tbsp olive oil (1 packet)

2 small or 1 large fresh lime(s)

4 small soft taco size tortillas

In a small spice bag:

1 tsp Old Bay seasoning blend

1 tsp granulated garlic

In a sandwich bag:

1 cup shredded cabbage (plain or tri-color with carrots)

Directions:
Heat the oil in your pan (or fry pan lid if you have one) over a low flame. Add in the spices and the tuna or salmon, gently heat through till sizzling, stirring often.
Divide between the tortillas, cut the lime(s) in half and squeeze over, top with cabbage as desired.

Serves 2

Notes:
Do you fish? For tasty fresh caught fish tacos, once you catch and clean your fish, prepare the fish in bite size chunks in the way you prefer – be it gently steamed or pan-fried and then proceed as above. This works great over a camp stove or a campfire. You will want to pack more oil though.

Like heated tortillas? Bring a piece of aluminum foil about 3 times as big as your tortillas (you can gently fold it at home to make it small). Before starting the fish, heat up your tortillas one at a time in a dry pan. Stash the hot tortillas in the foil, folding over like an envelope and they will keep warm while you cook!

Fresh cabbage is easy to carry while hiking and stays crisp for days. For ease, buy pre-shredded bags.

If you like salsa on your tacos you can pick up individual packets at www.minimus.biz

Herbed Tomato Rice

In a quart freezer or sandwich bag:

1 cup instant rice (white or brown)

¼ cup freeze-dried corn

¼ cup diced sun-dried tomatoes

1 Tbsp diced dried onion

1 ½ tsp lower sodium beef or chicken flavor bouillon

1 tsp granulated garlic

¼ tsp dried oregano

Also take:

1 Tbsp olive oil (1 packet)

2 sticks cheddar or pepper-jack cheese (2 ounces)

Directions:
FBC method:
Add 1 ½ cups near boiling water and the oil to the dry ingredients in a quart freezer bag. Seal tightly and tuck in a freezer bag cozy to insulate for 15 minutes.

One pot method:
Bring 1 ½ cups water and oil to a boil, add in the dry ingredients. Take off the heat and cover tightly. Let sit for 15 minutes (in cooler temperatures, or at altitude use a pot cozy to retain heat). Dice up the cheese and fold in.

Serves 2 as a side dish, alongside fish tacos.

Notes:
Find in the cheese sticks in the dairy aisle near the string cheese.

Lentil Soft Tacos

Ingredients:

½ cup instant rice

¼ cup cooked and dehydrated lentils

1 Tbsp diced dried bell peppers

1 Tbsp diced sun-dried tomatoes

1 Tbsp dried onion

1 tsp tomato powder

Pinch sugar

Pinch salt

Pinch granulated garlic

Also take:

1 packet True Lemon powder

2 soft taco size tortillas

1 oz queso fresco cheese

1 cup water

At home pack the instant rice in a pint freezer bag. Pack the remaining ingredients through garlic powder in a second pint freezer bag. Tuck in with the tortillas (wrapped in a sandwich bag or in plastic wrap). See notes below on the cheese.

FBC method:
Bring 1 cup water to a boil. Add ½ cup water to the rice bag, stir and seal tightly. Add ½ cup water to the lentil bag, stir well and seal tightly. Put both bags into a cozy for 15 minutes.

Crumble or dice the cheese and top the tortillas with the fillings, sprinkle the cheese on and fold over.

Serves 1

Notes:
True Lemon is found in most grocery stores, often with the sweeteners.

Find all the dried items online at www.harmonyhousefoods.com.

On the cheese: Queso Fresco can be found in most grocery stores, usually near the packaged sliced and shredded cheese. It comes in a wheel and crumbles easily. Use it for the first night out, if going on an extended trip you can carry cheddar or jack cheese, which carries better. For a vegan version of this recipe leave the cheese out.

Crab Mac n' Cheese

Pack in a quart plastic bag:

8 ounces uncooked macaroni

1 Tbsp dried onion

Pack in a sandwich bag:

1/2 cup dry milk

3 Tbsp all-purpose flour

1 Tbsp dried parsley

2 tsp dry mustard

1 tsp dried garlic

1/4 tsp ground black pepper

Also take:

8 ounce bag shredded sharp cheddar cheese

6 ounce can white crab meat

Directions:
In a 2 or 3 Liter pot bring 3 ½ cups water to a boil, add in the macaroni/onion and cook for time on pasta package, turning down the flame as needed to maintain a gentle boil.
Drain the crabmeat (the cans often have parchment paper in them, be sure to discard). When pasta is done (do not drain), turn the flame to very low and add in the seasoning bag and crabmeat, stir well. Turn off the stove and add about ¾ of the cheese, stir till melted. Taste for seasoning and add more pepper and or salt as desired (or a shake or two of hot sauce!).
Dish up and top with the remaining cheese.

Serves 2 large or 3 small portions

Pizza Biscuits

Pack in a gallon plastic bag:

1 cup all-purpose flour

3 Tbsp dry milk

1 Tbsp Italian herb blend

1 tsp baking powder

1/2 tsp dried garlic

1/2 tsp ground black pepper

1/4 tsp salt

Also take:

1 package shelf stable pepperoni

2 ounces string cheese (2 sticks)

2 Tbsp vegetable oil, in leak proof bottle

1 packet of pizza sauce (Boboli brand for example)

Directions:
Open up the bag and fold over making a "bowl". Dice up the cheese and add it and half the pepperoni to the bag along with ½ cup cool water, stir till mixed.
Heat a non-stick frying pan or shallow/wide pot over a medium flame, add half the oil and drop in small biscuit size of dough, flatten a bit and let cook till golden, flip over and cook till golden as well, lowering the stove's flame if cooking too fast.
Set aside and repeat with the remaining dough and oil.
Serve with the pizza sauce for dipping.

Makes about 6 biscuits, enough for 2 to 3

Notes:
The shelf stable pepperoni is found often with deli meat in grocery stores refrigerated but doesn't need to be kept cold until opened – it is noted on the label, Hormel is most common for brands. It comes with two separate inner packets, you need just one. Or look for Hormel's Mini Pepperoni slices (also shelf stable) and use half of the 5-ounce bag, planning the other half for breakfast or lunch the next day.

One Pot Chickpea Pasta

Ingredients:

4 oz spaghetti, broken into thirds

2 Tbsp cooked and dehydrated garbanzo beans

2 tsp lower sodium vegetable bouillon

¼ tsp granulated garlic

1 tsp dried parsley

Pinch red pepper flakes

¼ tsp ground black pepper

¼ cup shelf stable parmesan cheese

1 Tbsp olive oil (1 packet)

2 cups water

At home:
Pack the spaghetti in a sandwich bag. Put the beans through black pepper in a snack size bag and the Parmesan cheese in a second snack bag. Pack with the oil.

In camp:
Add the bean bag and oil to your pot with the water, let sit for 15 minutes.

Bring to a boil, add in the spaghetti and cook over a gentle boil for time on pasta package or until al dente. (There will be broth remaining).

Turn off your stove and add in the cheese, stirring well and let sit for a couple minutes to meld. Salt to taste if desired.

Serves 1

Notes:

Cooked and dried Garbanzo beans (chickpeas) can be found online at www.harmonyhousefoods.com.
For overnighters in cold weather you can also carry canned beans that you drain before leaving and carry in a zip top bag. Take at least ¼ cup or more and use first night out.

Blackberry Green Beans

Ingredients:

½ oz package freeze-dried green beans

½ tsp dried oregano

¼ tsp onion powder (not onion salt)

¼ tsp salt

¼ tsp ground black pepper

1-cup wild blackberries

1 cup boiling water

Directions:

As you hike pick the wild blackberries. A drinking cup or mug works well as a picking vessel.
Find and remove the oxygen absorber from the green bean package, add 1 cup boiling water and seal tightly. Let sit for 10 minutes.

Drain off any remaining water carefully. Sprinkle in the seasonings, gently toss. Very gently fold in the berries, let sit for a couple minutes for the juices to release.

Serves 2 as a side dish

Hiker's Primavera Pasta

Ingredients:

6 oz box white cheddar mac n' cheese

¼ cup freeze dried green peas

¼ cup freeze dried sweet corn

2 Tbsp diced dried carrots

2 Tbsp diced sun-dried tomatoes

¼ cup shelf stable parmesan cheese

1 Tbsp dry milk

1 tsp Italian herb seasoning

¼ tsp granulated garlic

¼ tsp freshly ground black pepper

1 Tbsp olive oil (1 packet)

4 cups water

At home:
In a sandwich bag pack the dry pasta and vegetables together. In a snack size bag pack the cheese sauce mix, cheese, dry milk and seasonings. Tuck the oil into a spill resistant container or use a convenient single serving packet.

Bring 4 cups water to a boil in your pot, add in the pasta bag and cook for time on package (usually 8 minutes). Reserve ¼ cup of the cooking water and drain the rest off carefully. Stir the seasoning bag into the pasta with the reserved water and oil till creamy.

Serves 2

Notes:

For the mac n' cheese we used Annie's natural brand. Any similar type will work - use the one you prefer.

Shelf stable Parmesan cheese? Look for the "green" cans.

Find the dried vegetables at www.harmonyhousefoods.com

Want it fresh for an overnighter in spring?
You can also make this dish with fresh vegetables! Pick up whatever items you like, a couple handfuls. Pea pods, baby zucchini, baby corn, work well. In camp, using a clean knife, chop up the items. Add to the boiling water with the pasta and continue as noted above. Finish the meal with a roma tomato chopped on top.

Spam-Tastic Fried Rice

Ingredients:

1 ½ cups instant rice

½ cups freeze-dried mixed vegetables

1 Tbsp dried chives

2 tsp lower sodium bouillon (veggie, beef or chicken)

½ tsp granulated garlic

¼ tsp dried powdered ginger

¼ tsp red pepper flakes

¼ tsp sugar

2 pkt soy sauce

3 oz Spam single packet

1 Tbsp vegetable oil (1 packet)

2 fresh eggs, in shell

2 cups water

At home:

Pack the rice, vegetables and all the seasonings in a quart freezer bag. Tuck the soy sauce, oil and Spam in with it.

Bring 2 cups water to a near boil. Add to the rice bag, stir well, seal tightly and put in a cozy for 15 minutes to rehydrate.

Heat the oil over a medium flame in a non-stick trail wok or 2 Liter pot and add in the Spam. Cube up and stir-fry till turning golden. Add in the cooked rice and stir constantly till smelling great. Splash on the soy sauce to taste and mix in.

Make a hole in the center and crack the eggs into it. Start scrambling them and then toss with the rice. Pull off the heat as soon as the eggs are setting up.

Serves 2

Notes:
Spam Singles are sold in the pouched/canned meat aisle. Find freeze-dried vegetables by Just Tomatoes at many local grocery stores and REI.
Fresh eggs carry well in the cooler months, just cut off part of a cardboard egg box and carry in your pot, padded with paper towels.

Lemon Tuna Spaghetti with Breadcrumbs

In a sandwich bag:

8 ounces spaghetti, broken into thirds

Also take:

1 Tbsp or 1 packet olive oil

1/4 cup pitted kalamata olives, chopped

3 Tbsp lemon juice (3 packets or 1 lemon)

2.6 to 3 ounce pouch Albacore or Light tuna

In a small bag:

1/4 cup seasoned breadcrumbs

1/4 cup shelf stable Parmesan cheese

1 tsp dried parsley

1/4 tsp ground black pepper

Directions:
In your pot, bring 4 cups water to boil. Add in the pasta and cook for time on package, drain carefully reserving ½ cup of the pasta water. Add in the oil, olives, lemon juice, tuna and reserved water to the pot, and toss to combine.
Sprinkle with breadcrumb mixture and toss again.

Serves 2

Notes:
For short trips carrying olives is fine, they are preserved. Use any pitted type from the olive bar! For longer trips or to save weight substitute freeze-dried olives (find at www.packitgourmet.com), add with the pasta to rehydrate.

Lemon juice packets and olive oil packets can be found online from www.minimus.biz. For lighter weight use 3 packets of True Lemon (found in the baking aisle at most stores) and 3 Tbsp water.

Last Minute Meat and Olive Pizzas

Ingredients:

1 twin pack 8" Boboli pizza shells

1 Boboli pizza sauce pouch (5-ounces)

½ package pepperoni slices (1 ½-ounces)

2 pieces string cheese (2 ounces)

8 olives of choice (from store olive bar)

2 Tbsp olive oil (or 2 packets)

2 paper towels

At home:
Pack the olive oil in a spill-proof bottle. Pick everything else up at your favorite grocery store on the way out of town. Carry the olives in a snack size zip top bag.

In camp:
Lay the paper towels down as a clean work surface. Divide the pizza sauce between the 2 shells, spreading it on the cheese side of the shell. Top each one with half of the pepperoni. With a clean knife, chop up the olives and cheese, and divide between the shells.
Using a wide fry pan lid or 2 Liter pot, heat it over a low flame. Add in half of the oil and carefully pop the pizza in. Cover tightly and let gently heat for 5 minutes. Keep an eye on it to prevent burning, lowering the flame as needed. Repeat for the second pizza.

Serves 2

Notes:
The shells start sizzling and poofing up when done. Let rest for a minute or so after taking off the heat before digging in.
String cheese carries well in your pack for a couple days. It will get soft and may be oily but is fine to use. Shelf stable pepperoni is sold in the pre-packed deli meat aisle - look for "refrigerate after opening" on the packaging, often near the expiration date. Each package has 2 packets, take one for this meal.

Many grocery stores have gourmet olive bars, choose whatever tasty ones you like, being sure to choose pitted ones. These are a great shelf stable treat when hiking.

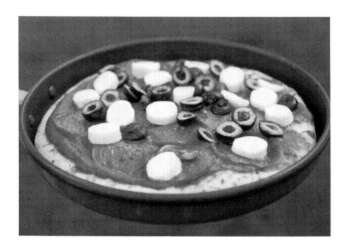

Harvest Pasta

Ingredients:

8 oz small pasta shapes (less than 7 min. cooking time)

1/3 cup diced sun-dried tomatoes

¼ cup crumbled dried mushrooms

1 tsp Italian herb seasoning

¼ tsp ground black pepper

¼ tsp red pepper flakes

½ cup shelf stable parmesan cheese

½ cup diced toasted walnuts

1 Tbsp olive oil (1 packet)

4 cups water

At home:
Pack the pasta and dried vegetables in a sandwich bag. In a second bag pack the seasonings through walnuts. Tuck the oil in.

In camp:
Bring the water to a boil in your pot, add in the pasta package. Cook for time on the pasta package. Take off the stove, drain off most of the remaining water, leaving a Tablespoon or so behind.
Toss the pasta with the olive oil and seasoning bag. Season to taste with extra salt and ground black pepper if desired.

Serves 2

Notes:

To save time and fuel look for pasta that cooks in less than 7 minutes. Both sun-dried tomatoes and mushrooms can be found in most grocery store produce departments, look up high and down low to find them!

Cherry Chicken Couscous

Ingredients:

1-cup couscous

½ cup diced dried cherries

1 Tbsp diced dried onion

1 tsp dried parsley

1 tsp true lime powder

½ tsp diced dried garlic

7 oz pouch chicken breast

1 Tbsp olive oil (1 packet)

1 ½ cups water

1 ½ tsp lower sodium chicken bouillon

Pack the dry ingredients in a quart freezer bag or a sandwich bag. Tuck the oil and chicken in with it.

One Pot method:
Bring 1 ½ cups water, oil and chicken with broth to a boil in your pot. Add in the dry ingredients, stir well, cover tightly and turn off the heat. Let sit for 10 minutes, fluff up.

Insulated mug method:
Add 1 ½ cups boiling water, oil and chicken with broth to the dry ingredients in a large mug. Stir well, cover tightly and let sit for 10 minutes. In cooler temperatures use a pot cozy to insulate. Fluff up.

Freezer bag method:
Add 1 ½ cups near boiling water, oil and chicken with broth to the bag. Stir well, seal tightly and put in a cozy for 10 minutes. Fluff up.

For all methods, fluff and add salt and black pepper to taste.

Serves 2

Notes:

True Lime powder is often found in the baking or sugar aisle of most grocery stores. Feel free to use True Lemon as well. Or pack a small lime and squeeze it in fresh.
For the couscous, use either regular or whole wheat for more protein. If you cannot find dried cherries, dried cranberries can be used.
For the chicken, look for 5-ounce cans with pop tops or preferably the easy to use 7 ounce pouches.

Harvest Rice

Ingredients:

1-cup instant rice

1-cup instant brown rice

½ cup freeze-dried vegetables

2 Tbsp homemade broth mix or 2 tsp lower sodium chicken bouillon

2 tsp dried parsley

Pinch of sea salt

Also take:

5 ounce can (w/ pop-top lid) or 7 ounce pouch chicken

1 Tbsp or packet olive oil

¼ cup finely chopped walnuts

At home:

Pack the rice ingredients in a sandwich bag or quart freezer bag, depending on cooking method. Mark "Add 2 ½ cups water" on bag. Pack the walnuts in a snack bag.

One Pot Method:

Add the chicken, with any broth, water and oil to a cooking pot. Bring to boil, add the rice bag, return to boil. Turn off the stove, cover tightly and let sit for 15 minutes. In cooler weather or at altitude insulate the pot with a pot cozy.

Stir the rice, top with the walnuts.

Freezer Bag Method (FBC):

Bring the water to a boil, set aside. Place the freezer bag in a cozy, add the oil and chicken, with any broth and the water. Stir well, seal and let sit for 15 minutes.

To make a second 'bowl' bring along a second freezer bag, cuff in half.

Divide the rice and top with the walnuts.

Serves 2

Cheery Cherry Pasta Salad

Ingredients:

2 cups lower sodium vegetable broth

1 ½ cups couscous

15 ounce can chickpeas (garbanzo beans), rinsed and drained

¼ cup dried cherries

¼ cup sliced almonds, toasted and cooled

Dressing:

¼ cup red wine vinegar

¼ cup extra virgin olive oil

1 Tbsp agave nectar or honey

1 tsp dry parsley

½ tsp ground black pepper

¼ tsp salt, if desired

Directions:
Bring the broth to a boil in a medium saucepan, add in the couscous. Take off the heat, cover tightly and let sit for 10 minutes. Fluff up the couscous with a fork into a large bowl, toss with the chickpeas, cherries and almonds.

Whisk the dressing in a small bowl, taste for seasoning. Pour the dressing over and toss to coat. Let chill overnight and then pack into lightweight sandwich containers with tight-fitting lids.

Makes 2-3 large portions

Nettle Pesto Pasta

Ingredients:

8 oz pasta of choice, cook time under 7 minutes

¼ cup toasted finely diced pine nuts or walnuts

½ cup shelf stable parmesan cheese

1 cup extra virgin olive oil

1 cup packed stinging nettle leaves (urtica dioica)

1 ¼ tsp granulated garlic

At home:
Pack the pasta in a sandwich bag, the nuts and garlic in a small bag, the Parmesan cheese in a snack bag and the olive oi in a leak proof container.

In camp:
In your pot bring a ¼ cup water to a boil, add your nettle leaves, cover tightly and let steam a couple minutes (lower your stove's flame). Drain off any water left, then chop the leaves as finely as you can. Add the olive oil to the nut bag, then add the nettles. Stir well and put aside.

Bring 4 cups water to a boil in your pot, add the pasta and cook for time on package. Drain carefully. Add pesto to pasta as desired, top liberally with the cheese.

The sauce can also be made at home, process in a blender or food processor till smooth. Feel free to use fresh Parmesan cheese if done this way.

Notes:
When picking nettle leaves DO wear gloves and a long sleeved shirt. A clean freezer bag is a good picking vessel.

DESSERTS

Pumpkin and Gingersnap Pudding

Ingredients:

2/3 cup dry milk

¼ cup brown sugar, packed

3 Tbsp cornstarch or favorite thickener, arrowroot works as well

2 Tbsp dried and powdered pumpkin puree (see below)

½ tsp ground cinnamon

Big pinch ground nutmeg

Big pinch ground ginger

Big pinch salt

Also take:

1 Tbsp unsalted butter

1 bag crisp gingersnap cookies (7-9 ounces)

At home:

Pack the pudding ingredients in a sandwich bag. Tuck the butter in a small bag.

One Pot Method:

Add the mix and 2 cups cold water to a cooking pot. Using a small whisk, stir while bringing to boil, over a lower flame. When the pudding comes to a boil and is thick, take off the stove and whisk in the butter. Serve warm or let cool, a cold stream or snow bank works well for chilling.

Divide between mugs or bowls, or in a pinch served in pint freezer bags.

Crumble up some of the gingersnaps, dust on top, and serve with the rest to dip in the pudding.

Serves 2 to 4, depending on appetite

Notes:

Dried pumpkin? Very easy! Spread a can of organic pumpkin puree on a parchment paper lined baking sheet, dehydrate in your oven at lowest temp till dry, then powder. Store tightly sealed. See http://www.trailcooking.com/dehydrating-101/vegetables/ on how to do it in a dehydrator.

Want it even better? Add in a splash of rum at the end, after it comes off the stove.

Double Ginger Huckleberry Cobbler

Ingredients:

2/3 cup baking mix

1 Tbsp sugar

1 Tbsp diced candied ginger

¼ tsp dry ginger powder

¼ cup white sugar

2 Tbsp corn starch

¼ tsp true lime or lemon powder

1 cup fresh huckleberries

1 ¼ cup water

At home:
Pack the baking mix (i.e.:Bisquick®), 1 Tbsp sugar and the two gingers in a quart or sandwich bag. Pack the ¼ cup sugar, corn starch and True Lime in a snack bag.

In camp:
Pick about 1 cup fresh Huckleberries, making sure stems are plucked off. That is about 4 handfuls of berries.

Add ¼ cup cool water to the baking mix bag and knead gently till mixed. Seal and set aside.

Add 1-cup water to your pot and stir in the small sugar bag till dissolved. Add in the berries and bring the pot to a boil. Lower the flame on your stove to as low as it will go and quickly add in the prepared baking mix by dropping in spoonfuls on the hot berry mixture. Put on the pot's lid and simmer gently on low heat for 10 to 12 minutes or until the topping is done.

Serves 2

Pina Colada Mini Pies

Ingredients:

2/3 cup dry milk

1 6-pack mini graham cracker crusts

¼ cup finely chopped candied pecans

¼ cup sweetened flaked coconut

1 Tbsp rum (if desired)

1 ¾ cups cold water

1 4-serving carton instant cheesecake pudding mix

At home:
Pack the pudding mix and milk in a quart freezer bag. Mark "Add 1 ¾ cups water" on the bag. Pack individually the pecans and coconut in snack size bags. Keep the mini piecrusts in their packaging to protect them. If taking rum pick up a 1-ounce bottle from the liquor store.

In camp:
Add 1 ¾ cups very cold water to the pudding mix. Seal the bag tightly and shake for a couple minutes. This is a great thing for little ones to help with! Stash the bag of pudding in a cold creek or snow bank to chill 15 to 30 minutes (go eat dinner!).
Cut off a corner of the bag and pipe the pudding into the 6 mini crusts. Sprinkle the nuts in the center and the coconut around the outside.

Serves 2 to 6, depending on appetite

Berry Dessert

In a sandwich bag pack:

¼ cup sugar

1 Tbsp cornstarch or arrowroot flour

1 tsp ground cinnamon

1 tsp dried lemon zest

Also take:

1 Tbsp butter or margarine

Cake of choice for topping (pound cake, desert cups, angel food cake, Twinkies, etc)

Pick 2 cups Huckleberries, Blueberries or Blackberries while hiking or in camp.

Directions:

Add the dry ingredients to your pot, stir in 2 Tablespoons cool water and add the berries. Place the butter on top and over a very low flame on your stove bring the mixture to a gentle boil, stirring often.

Once thickened, take off the stove and serve with your choice of cake.

Serves 2

Notes:
For a lighter weight version (and ability to carry long-term) substitute 1 Tablespoon butter powder. Butter powder can be found in specialty kitchen shops, online (www.packitgourmet.com) or you can use Molly McButter/Butter Buds, found in the spice aisle at grocery stores. Dried lemon zest is also found in the spice aisle. A small fresh lemon carried and squeezed in is a gourmet touch.

Low Fat Fudgy Brownies

Ingredients:

½ cup all-purpose flour

½ cup unsweetened cocoa powder

½ cup packed brown sugar

1/8 tsp kosher salt

1 Tbsp olive oil

4-ounce jar or tub of stage 2 baby applesauce

½ cup canned pumpkin purée

2 tsp pure vanilla extract

Directions:
Preheat the oven to 350°F and spray an 8×8" glass baking pan with cooking spray.
In a medium bowl whisk the dry ingredients together.
In a large bowl whisk the wet ingredients together. Add the dry to the wet, stir or whisk until combined.
Spread into the prepared baking dish and bake for 20 to 25 minutes, checking at 20, until a toothpick in the center comes out mostly clean (moist crumb but not wet dough).
Let cool and cut. Carry in small plastic bags or wrapped in plastic wrap. Eat within 2 days of baking for best results.

Notes:

To carry a picnic lunch easily, acquire a lightweight children's insulated lunch bag (found at all big box stores). Pack ice cubes in quart freezer bags, double bagged. Your lunch will stay cold and after lunch you will have ice-cold water/ice to add to your water bottle!

Add in a couple of paper napkins, spoons, some crunchy fresh veggies (baby carrots and pea pods are great) and your favorite drink mix – and a scenic lunch spot and enjoy lunch.

Mocha Pudding

Ingredients:

1 4-serving carton instant chocolate pudding mix

2/3 cup dry milk

1 tsp espresso powder

2 cups cold water

¼ cup glazed pecans

At home:
Pack the pudding mix, dry milk and espresso powder in a quart freezer bag. Tuck the pecans in a small bag.

In camp:
Add the cold water to the pudding bag. Seal tightly and shake for 2 minutes or use a spoon or whisk to beat it. Park the pudding in a cold stream or snowbank to finish setting up for 30 minutes or so, or until you have eaten dinner and crave dessert!

Divide up and top with pecans.

Serves 2 to 4

Ice Cream in a Bag!

Ingredients:

1 new gallon size freezer bag

2 new quart size freezer bags

¾ cup rock salt

1/3 cup dry milk

2 Tbsp sugar

For flavor ideas:
2 packets of jam or preserves (2 Tbsp)
1 tsp extract of choice (vanilla, coconut, almond, maple, etc)
Add-ins: mini chocolate chips, coconut, berries, etc. - a Tablespoon or two.

At home:
Pack the rock salt into the gallon freezer bag and seal tightly. In a quart freezer bag, pack the dry milk and sugar and any dry add-ins if you are using them. Seal bag tightly. If using jam or liquid extracts, pack separately.

In camp:
Add 1-cup very cold water (think snow fed stream) to the dry milk bag and gently shake to dissolve. Add in any flavorings or jam and if using add-ins, those also, push the air out of the bag and seal tightly. If you are worried about any chance of the bag opening double bag it in a second quart freezer bag.

Open the gallon freezer bag and fill the bag at least halfway with snow. Dense icy snow is best. Toss in the milk bag, seal tightly and find a small child or bored campmate to shake the bag back and forth for 10 minutes.

Open up the outer bag and take the ice cream bag out. Pour some cold water over the outside of the bag to rinse the salt off, open up, stir and dig in!

Serves 1 to 2 or more if you share

Notes:

For a more decadent treat use NIDO© full fat dry milk, found at many grocery stores, Wal-Mart and Hispanic grocery stores. Most dry milk is non-fat.

For a wide variety of single serving packets of jam and preserves visit www.minimus.biz or save extras from breakfast out. You can also pack jam into a small container or snack size zip top bag for carrying.

Double Oreo© Pudding

In a quart freezer bag:

1 4-serving package Jell-o Oreo Cookies 'n Creme© instant pudding

2/3 cup dry milk

Also take:

1 8 ounce package Mini Oreos©

2-3 new snack size bags

Directions:
Add 2 cups cold water to the pudding bag, seal tightly and shake for 5 minutes. Stash in a cold stream or snow bank for 30 minutes. Stir up and divide between the bags. Top liberally with mini cookies.

Serves 2-3

Notes:

Find the Mini Oreos© in the cookie aisle at all grocery stores, they come in Mylar bags for easy packing. For a more decadent pudding use full fat Nido© dry milk instead of the usual non-fat dry.

About The Author

Sarah lives in a small, but growing, town in the foothills of Mt. Rainier, in Washington State, with her husband Kirk, and three sons, Ford, Walker, and Alistaire.
She is the author of Freezer Bag Cooking: Trail Food Made Simple, Trail Cooking: Trail Food Made Gourmet and Oats Gone Wild.
Her favorite hiking areas are the Washington Cascade Mountains and Mount Rainier National Park.
She can be found online at www.gazingin.com, www.trailcooking.com and http://blog.trailcooking.com/ and on Facebook at www.facebook.com/pages/Freezer-Bag-Cooking/ and Twitter at https://twitter.com/trailcooking.
If you have any questions or comments, please email her at sarah@trailcooking.com.

© 2011 Matthew Kirkconnell

Made in the USA
San Bernardino, CA
25 November 2014